First World War
and Army of Occupation
War Diary
France, Belgium and Germany

28 DIVISION
Divisional Troops
Royal Army Medical Corps
84 Field Ambulance
2 January 1915 - 31 October 1915

WO95/2272/5

The Naval & Military Press Ltd
www.nmarchive.com
Published in association with The National Archives

Published by

The Naval & Military Press Ltd

Unit 10 Ridgewood Industrial Park,

Uckfield, East Sussex,

TN22 5QE England

Tel: +44 (0) 1825 749494

www.naval-military-press.com

www.nmarchive.com

This diary has been reprinted in facsimile from the original. Any imperfections are inevitably reproduced and the quality may fall short of modern type and cartographic standards.

© **Crown Copyright**
Images reproduced by permission of The National Archives, London, England, 2015.

Contents

Document type	Place/Title	Date From	Date To
Heading	WO95/2272/5		
Heading	28th Division Medical 84th Fld Ambulance Jan-Oct 1915		
Heading	28th Division 84th Field Ambulance Vol I 2-31.1.15		
War Diary	Hursley Winchester	02/01/1915	02/01/1915
War Diary	Winchester	03/01/1915	15/01/1915
War Diary	La Havre	16/01/1915	17/01/1915
War Diary	On Train	18/01/1915	18/01/1915
War Diary	La Balle Croix	20/01/1915	31/01/1915
Heading	84th Field Ambulance Vol II		
War Diary	In The Field	01/02/1915	28/02/1915
Heading	84th Field Ambulance Vol III		
War Diary	In The Field	01/03/1915	31/03/1915
Heading	84th Field Ambulance Vol IV		
War Diary	Ypres	01/04/1915	11/04/1915
War Diary	Poperinghe	12/04/1915	30/04/1915
Heading	28th Division 84th Field Ambulance Vol V May 1915		
War Diary	Poperinghe	01/05/1915	07/05/1915
War Diary	Wippenhoek Farm Ref. Sq Map 27 Belgium L.28.D.5.5	08/05/1915	30/05/1915
Heading	28th Division 84th Field Ambulance Vol VI June 1915		
War Diary	Winnezeele	01/06/1915	30/06/1915
Heading	28th Division 84th Field Ambulance Vol VII From 1st To 31st July 1915		
War Diary	La Clytte	01/07/1915	15/07/1915
War Diary	Boeschepe	16/07/1915	31/07/1915
Heading	28th Division 84th Field Ambulance Vol VIII August 15		
War Diary		01/08/1915	31/08/1915
Heading	28th Division 84th Field Ambulance Vol IX Sept 15		
War Diary		01/09/1915	30/09/1915
Heading	28th Div. 84 (2nd/12) Fd. Amb Oct Vol X Oct 1915		
War Diary		01/10/1915	31/10/1915

moss / 2272(5)

moss / 2272(5)

28TH DIVISION
MEDICAL

84TH FLD AMBULANCE
JAN-OCT 1915

28th Division.

121/4447

84th Field Ambulance.

Vol I. 2 - 31.1.15.

Jan 1915.

Army Form C. 2118.

85" Field Ambulance
Late 2nd London

WAR DIARY
or
INTELLIGENCE SUMMARY.
(Erase heading not required.)

Instructions regarding War Diaries and Intelligence Summaries are contained in F.S. Regs., Part II. and the Staff Manual respectively. Title pages will be prepared in manuscript.

Hour, Date, Place	Summary of Events and Information	Remarks and references to Appendices
1915		
2nd Jan. Thursday Winchester	Orders received to move into billets at Winchester tomorrow	
Sunday 3rd Jan.	Moved into billets at St Cross. Winchester. Church Parade	
4	Slept at "St Theatre" Ford W.	
	Went out equipt began to arrive	
6	Entrainment completed in horses & vehicles	
7	New Med. equipt arrived	
9	Inspection Officer med. equip. Southwark	
11	Orders rec'd for H.M. the Kings inspection of div. tomorrow	
12	Inspected by H.M. the King & Lord Kitchener	
	H. Reynolds exchanged with Pts. Late Humbershank left for Aldershot to exchange to Recon on	
13	All kits stores returned to Ordnance of to Repair supplies	
14	gas string. Saddles re. left personal equipped to personnel by a party from Northumberland Fus. Ambulance	
	Marched from Winchester 10.20 am to Southampton	
15	Arr. S'ton 1.30 pm took 2.30 pm S.S. Tintoretto	
	Embarked men horses/vehicles on S.S. Tintoretto	
	Cleared pier/took 6.30 pm. After all night arrived	
16 Lethavre	Le Havre off 6.30 am very rough passage.	
	Lay off Lethavre till about 11 a.m. sea very rough. Men both were light not comfortable. Disembarked	
	troops & horses & vehicles marched arrival with	

Army Form C. 2118.

8th Field Ambulance
Lieut. Col. W. H. Sanders

WAR DIARY
or
INTELLIGENCE SUMMARY.
(Erase heading not required.)

Instructions regarding War Diaries and Intelligence Summaries are contained in F. S. Regs., Part II. and the Staff Manual respectively. Title pages will be prepared in manuscript.

Hour, Date, Place	Summary of Events and Information	Remarks and references to Appendices
1915 16 Jan. Le Havre	Marched out of Dockyard about 5 to No 2 Camp at Bleville about 1-4 miles. Very old roads, but the road of the range had dust.	
17 Jan.	Soon after 1 a.m. received orders to entrain at 9 a.m. Merchandise point 3 at 12 noon. Sergt W. Harwood & Interpreter (Ashford) paid to clearing Chief kin., easy to the road ends all suspense. Marched from Camp received sharp to time. Had good appreciation in entraining to manoeuvring of vehicle trucks with all hand- own to manoeuvring of vehicle trucks with all hand- till train time finally. Left 2 ambulance wagons behind at the station. Separated at 3.20 p.m. Travelled all day until night lit. via Rouen Abbeville Boulogne Calais. Reached St Omer abt 3.15 p.m. on the 18th noon after 10 minutes halt. travel where entrained at about 4.30 or 5 pm. nearly 3 hours work delivering at Juliaustaine. Stated Received instructions to march to Juliaustaine. Arrived (off 18 miles) the road – 10 miles distant. Arrived (off 18 miles) Shortly after 1 a.m. received orders to join La Belle Croix abt 1½ mile further. Arrived abt 2. new line thoroughly exhausted. Pitched dark, stinking, & mud kneels with black. very narrow site	
18 Jan on Train		

Army Form C. 2118.

89 Field Ambulance
late 3rd Battalion

WAR DIARY
or
INTELLIGENCE SUMMARY.
(Erase heading not required.)

Instructions regarding War Diaries and Intelligence Summaries are contained in F. S. Regs., Part II. and the Staff Manual respectively. Title pages will be prepared in manuscript.

Hour, Date, Place	Summary of Events and Information	Remarks and references to Appendices
1915		
2.0 am La Bellotte	Sent Lt Hayne & staff ahead of Main body. Then Capt Bickerton attached to M. Jules Vandervelles Farm with tent sub div of C. Section for hospital duty.	
	Lt Hayne ordered A Section & 10 horses detached to M. Lalays farm for hospital & above Corporal at La Belle Croix	
24	Church Parade at Maison Rachuad.	
26	Lt Coutauld appointed Sanitary Officer for Taylors billets in 83rd Brigade area.	
27	Orders received to stand by ready for short tactical move.	
28	Inspected with 83rd Bde by C in C.	
29	Moved to Y—	
30	Lt Copitol billets &Apph	
31	Started with most of Main south except Capt. Grimsley & G— room to come on tomorrow by bus. Having reached C— Island both with some Officers men to wait for Governour's Convoy.	

Wm Salisbury Sharpe
Lt Col.

84th Casualty Field Ambulance

Vol II.

Army Form C. 2118.

84th (Second Wessex) Field Ambulance
28 Division

WAR DIARY
or
INTELLIGENCE SUMMARY.
(Erase heading not required.)

Instructions regarding War Diaries and Intelligence Summaries are contained in F.S. Regs., Part II. and the Staff Manual respectively. Title pages will be prepared in manuscript.

Hour, Date, Place	Summary of Events and Information	Remarks and references to Appendices
IN THE FIELD		
1915 February 1st	Went on motor buses from Wulver via Corbie Steenwoorde & Poperinghe. Marched from Shrapnel Cnr to Ypres. Riding School stopped by French horse. 3 joint men into Gymnasium & Dressing Stn. Officers (in 3 rooms) Post men and Cavalry Bks B attached hospital with all the quartermaster's men at Hosp'l in billet B010	
2nd	Started accommodation for sick at 21-Jan. filled up 45 beds 8 sick	
3rd	Reg'n for officers sleep'g qtrs & Y.M. mess room for Sun & Jerh	
4th	Re conditioning by G.O. discharge of under emptation of Hosp. down with Capt.	
5th		
6th	Over 100 casualties. Orders received. Our movement to Yperlee to Ambleve.	
7th	Will stand fast. Gym very late. Total Casualties 108.	
8th	Casualties 120. O very bad. Self-inflicted on suspected, rifle-shot wounds to Casualties 36 the Arm re pending [inquiry?]. Notify to R.A.M.C.	
9th	Quel hosp'l Yours reported in improvement walked at Rosier Station	
10th	Ordered 13 Jul up to discharged belof'g for Christian and Paris. Cresulties 94.	
11th	D then B98 Cresu. T.B.R. land of hosp'l the. Many sick returned to Hosp 8 5 T.	
	N. Camp, R.A.M.C. acres 96 re-admitted 105. Many man Sick 18 8 5 T.	
12th	French hospitals Bath. B. ad Adv. F Drs 113. Osp. 113. with	
	retiring to bath in rotation. Casualties 147.	
13th	Wise Johnsoncth arrived 84th. D.Stone Col. Prt of the T casualties.	
	Gorm followin hospital. Sour form of deaf state. Callbells took with.	
	Casualties 80.	
14th	S then arrived no Records wood writing 7 Nurses 4 Orderlies Casualties 52	

84 (2nd London) Field Ambulance

Army Form C. 2118.

WAR DIARY
or
INTELLIGENCE SUMMARY.
(Erase heading not required.)

Hour, Date, Place	Summary of Events and Information	Remarks and references to Appendices
1915 February		
15th	Casualties 182	
16	Major Montgomery Smith removed ill. Casualties 261.	
17	Evacuation Station started. Took C.R.E. to Water tank & round around to 85?	
	Casualties 2	
18	Detail under major shelling hard: many lamps "took jn water"	
	Better outer majority section dutier "took jn water"	
	Both t'evant went to A.D.M.S	
	Casualties 221	
19	Casualties 266. Pte Ward wounded in abdomen. near Bertenhurt	
	Turnbull wound.	
20	At Midnight Nestor sent Lt C. Noth Zavierty	
	Pte Gillmouth killed in France. Casualties 157	
21	Sensation. Ambulance very good work. Eight might out by ghost. instants	
	Casualties 277.	
22	2nd Farmer Jewish. Casualties 176	
23	Casualties 19	
24	Pte Sparks 89 Fld artod. Casualties 26	
25	Casualties 8-9	
26	Pte Porter killed in ac. Casualties 57	
27	Casualties 99	
28	Head cook Officer Holroyd? town out sanches. Casualties 72.	
	Total Casualties for the month 3680.	

Wm Salisbury Sharpe Lt Col

12/4/49

84th Field Ambulance
Vol III

12/1919 15
March 1915

Army Form C. 2118.

8th Field Ambulance

WAR DIARY
or
INTELLIGENCE SUMMARY.
(Erase heading not required.)

Instructions regarding War Diaries and Intelligence Summaries are contained in F.S. Regs., Part II. and the Staff Manual respectively. Title pages will be prepared in manuscript.

Hour, Date, Place	Summary of Events and Information	Remarks and references to Appendices
In the Field 19/1/15 March 1.	Detailed inspection Everything by A.D.M.S. Canadian S. with 60 Total 3. Wounded 54. Total 117.	
2.	Canadian S.67. F.2. W.46. = Total 115. Canadian S. with 60	
3.	S.44. F.1. W.38. = Total 83.	
4.	Afghans 8. U.K. S.24. F.41. W.103 Total 176	
5.	S.34. F.0. W.37 = Total 71.	
6.	S.26. F.2. W.34 = Total 62	
7.	S.21. F.0. W.12 = Total 33.	
8.	S.39. F.2. W.31 = Total 72	
8a	N.O. arrived. D. General's Appreciation Quote Afghans. Sunday squad Director now with wagon details established reporting Pelthem (17065) arrived Antwerp Newgate	
9.	Reported Paper stockings. Kept at B.O.B. de Vistation Begin. Casualties. S.13. F.8. W.25 = Total 46.	
10.	21 Hospital moved up from Ath.M.D. Order to make a "medical" word at B. is temper Posh.	
	Casualties. S.27. F.1. W.41 = Total 69.	
11.	S.21. F.1. W.23 = 45. Keep Bunabies	
12.	S.35. F.1. W.25 = 61	
13.	S.25. F.0. W.34 = 59	(Hd

2/7 Field Ambulance

Army Form C. 2118.

WAR DIARY
or
INTELLIGENCE SUMMARY.
(Erase heading not required.)

Hour, Date, Place	Summary of Events and Information	Remarks and references to Appendices
1915		
March 14	Lt Turnbull died. Battle of N[eu]ve Chap[elle].	
	Casualties 8.41. F 2 W 99 = Total 142 A very bad day	
15	3.26. F 3 W 34 = 63	
16	8.54. F 1 W 34 = 99	
17	8.15. F 0 W 22 = 37	
18	Reinforcement of 1 offr & 9 men arrived	
	Casualties S.11. F.0. W 25 = 36	
19	SNOW. Casualties 8.16. F.0. W.17 = Total 33.	
20	V. smite ??? S(?)andbags &c with A.D.M.S fine day but	
	C.W. Snow in evg. Casualties S.22 F 0 W.22 = 44	
21	Casualties S. 26. F.1. W.2.2. = Total 49.	
22	8.50 F.1. W. 18 = 69.	
23	3.28 F.0 W. 11 = 39	
24	A.D.M.S called to see Isolation ward & patients	
	Sent 26. convoid R.E.s to Braudhock [orthotic?] Advanced	
	action were S.T. patients. Casualties S. 30. F 2 W.19 = 51	
25	Raining most of day. Resume infectious cases notes	
	received that 2.9. is moving tomorrow	
	Casualties S.31. F 1 W 11 = Total 43	
26	S. 18. F. 1 W.18 = 37	
27	S.35. F.0 W.12 = 47	

84 Field Ambulance

WAR DIARY
or
INTELLIGENCE SUMMARY.
(Erase heading not required.)

Army Form C. 2118.

Hour, Date, Place	Summary of Events and Information	Remarks and references to Appendices
1915 March 28th	Casualties S.20 F.O W.18 = Total 38 S.21 F.O W.11 = 32 S.11 F.1 W.14 = 26 S.8 F.O W.15 = 23	During the month against total Sp Sanitary work was done YPRES. & the military water supply. Nevertheless great work continued during the month also. The French garrison commenced shower for the men supply. Shellowed daily water to the town, but no great harm was done to our establishments.
29th		
30th		
31st	Total Casualties admitted during the month 1917.	W. Salisbury Sharp Lt Col

121/5321

14/5321
April 1915

84th Field Ambulance

Vol IV

Army Form C. 2118.

84 (Second London) Field Ambulance
28 Div B.E.F.

WAR DIARY
or
INTELLIGENCE SUMMARY.
(Erase heading not required.)

Instructions regarding War Diaries and Intelligence Summaries are contained in F.S. Regs., Part II. and the Staff Manual respectively. Title pages will be prepared in manuscript.

Hour, Date, Place	Summary of Events and Information	Remarks and references to Appendices
YPRES 1915 April 1st	Casualties S.14 W.31 Total 45	
2	" 19 " 10 " 29	
3	" 23 " 17 " 40	
4th	" 25 " 19 " 44 — Good Friday. Visit of Bishop of London & service in Gymnasium 2.15. Easter Sunday. First orders to hand over tomorrow to 1/2d Dvn Amb of the 15th Fd Amb. Town heavily bombarded at 9 & 9 p.m. Three shells struck St Elizabeth. Coming through the main's billets collected this two 10 & 12 inch. & one 6 inch. Killed two men wounded six.	
5th	2 Received Bayonet Knights. moved from all posts in YPRES to billets at Asylum. Handing over to 15 Fd Amb. together with A.S.M. Went	
6th	Inspected other quarters in town. afternoon	
7	Recd orders to proceed to POPERINGHE	
8th	Went to P. to obtain billets. Marched in 2 Offrs. 3 NCOs & 30 men to prepare quarters. Capt Radford rejoined.	
9th	Marched to POPERINGHE. Revd Campbell left. Evan killed at 22 Rue St.	
10th	in boys school Rue de Bassin. Officers in private houses.	
11	Hewitt & Motor Transport and orderlies.	

Smyth Forms/C. 2118/10.

Army Form C. 2118.

84th (Second London) Field Ambulance
28 Div B.E.F

WAR DIARY
or
INTELLIGENCE SUMMARY.
(Erase heading not required.)

Instructions regarding War Diaries and Intelligence Summaries are contained in F.S. Regs., Part II. and the Staff Manual respectively. Title pages will be prepared in manuscript.

Hour, Date, Place	Summary of Events and Information				Remarks and references to Appendices
1915		W	=	Total	
POPERINGHE April 12th	Casualties	1	=	1	Aeroplane bombardment at 6:30 am & at 5:pm. Road order att. Sunday. supervision photos by Brigdr. Standard took over Convent & Rest from 85th
13th		11	0	11.	Sang 6 am Conf. Stand convalescent rest station
14th		15	0	15	Inspected. Conf. atho. Withs. Water supplies
15th		59	5	64	Recd. Orders to prepare for & open
16th		36	2	38	Visited on firing line all night. Irnwt with B.A.D.M.S. to ZONNEBEKE to the road & and park.
17th		35	0	35.	
18th		15	4	19	Stated B. Stations Extern. Goudeserk Boesinghe
19th		22	2	24.	Inspecting whole Front line by Brita. A.D.M.S came in Mr. Say Gun in Aft YPRES
20th		59	26	85	
21		23	1	24	
22		24	14	38.	Heavy fighting at YPRES. recommenced
23		4	7	11.	Collecting work heavy
24		12	532	544	
25th		10	154	164	Bombardment of POPERINGHE with 6 inch Shells
26th		14	68	82	" " " 12 " " "
27th		2	75	77	more 12 inch shells
28th		8	138	146	"3 from new inward"
29		82	189	271	
30					
Total for Month				1821	

Wmlalubing Shurte
Lt Col

121/5775

28th Division

84 to Field Ambulance
Vol VI

121/5775

May 1915
S/

Army Form C. 2118.

84th (2nd London) Field Ambulance C
28th Division

WAR DIARY
or
INTELLIGENCE SUMMARY.
(Erase heading not required.)

Instructions regarding War Diaries and Intelligence Summaries are contained in F.S. Regs., Part II. and the Staff Manual respectively. Title pages will be prepared in manuscript.

Hour, Date, Place	Summary of Events and Information	Remarks and references to Appendices
MAY 1915 POPERINGHE. Occupying Brig: command school — Rue St Bertin. Bearer W/o Sparre distributed in 1st, Bar to Bangs, and hugeing station in 17 Rue d'YPRES.		
1st.	Collecting from North front of YPRES Salient, via aid posts at POLYGON WOOD, ST JEAN, POTIZTE, ZONNEBEKE, ST JULIEN, and at a point about half way between the cross-roads W.N.W. of FORTUIN and GRAVENSTAFEL. Casualties:— Sick 71, Wounded 281, Total 352.	
2nd.	First "gas" cases received. Following an unsuccessful [?] attack by (1) Shropshire (3) Shropshire (4) Pollution (5) Devonshire (6) [?] of some (7) [?] and (8) Durham & [?] (9) Sherwood, attacked. Most of these appeared to get some temporary relief, but none held any apparent [?] to mitigate permanently a bad case. Casualties: Sick 80, Gas 414, Wounded 495. Total 989.	
3rd.	[?] J I LAWSON reported. Casualties:— Sick 97, Gas 292, Wounded 625. Total 1,014.	
4th.	[?] put on duty in [?] and tying of [?] we are to [?] a [?] at any time. Casualties: Sick 107, Gas 115, Wounded 317. Total 539.	
5th.	Casualties: Sick 85, Gas 95, Wounded 410, Total 634.	
6th.	Casualties [?] 105 [?] 3 [?] 163 [?] 271.	

Army Form C. 2118.

WAR DIARY
or
INTELLIGENCE SUMMARY.
(Erase heading not required.)

8th (2nd London) Field Ambulance
28th Division

Instructions regarding War Diaries and Intelligence Summaries are contained in F. S. Regs., Part II. and the Staff Manual respectively. Title pages will be prepared in manuscript.

Hour, Date, Place	Summary of Events and Information	Remarks and references to Appendices
MAY 1915		
7th	Field Ambulance moved to WIPPENHOEK Farm N. of N. of ag ag aj Belgium L28 D55 lotting where continued and "C" section left at POPERINGHE the following my: Casualties - Sick 23. Wounded 9. Total 42.	
WIPPENHOEK Farm 8th N of ag ag aj Belgium L28 D55	"C" section left POPERINGHE and came to WIPPENHOEK. Tent division of "B" section returned to temple at POPERINGHE to stand by, ready for open up of Munday.	
9th	Lolling duties continued	
10th	Transport to Motor Ambulance Con - Dodiry and two trivias engaged. "C" Tent subdivision relieved "B" section afternoon. made.	
11th	Lieut. W. BAXTER temporarily detached. Rev. C J DANBURY Left "C" Tent sub division returned leaving on NCO and two men as guard on Stories.	
12th	Rev. C J RADFORD left; Rev FARNFIELD joined.	
13th	Special orders by A-G. inspecting Officers Rila	
14th	Field Ambulance moved to VANDERLYNN Farm, at LE TEMPLE near WINNEZEELE. "B" section to LE CROOQ Farm at WINNEZEELE to receive Brigade sick.	
15th	Lieut CROSS N. temporarily detached. Battalion of 83rd Brigade instructed on use of Vermorel Sprayer. Casualties - Sick 4.	

WAR DIARY
INTELLIGENCE SUMMARY.
(Erase heading not required.)

Army Form C. 2118.

Instructions regarding War Diaries and Intelligence Summaries are contained in F.S. Regs., Part II. and the Staff Manual respectively. Title pages will be prepared in manuscript.

84th (2nd London) Field Ambulance
2nd London Division

Hour, Date, Place	Summary of Events and Information	Remarks and references to Appendices
MAY 1915		
16th	Lieut W BAXTER rejoined. Casualties - Sick 8.	
17th	Instructions received for disposal of effects of deceased Belgian soldiers. Stretcher & slings ordered with to be overhauled by bearers as personal equipment. Casualties - Sick 12.	
18th	Casualties - Sick 9. Wounded 1. Total 10	
19th	Casualties - Sick 5.	
20th	25% of khakis overhauled. Information respecting poisoning of streams by enemy, and instructions as regards bandaging "Casualties" Sick 14.	
21st	Casualties Sick 22. Wounded 2. Total 24.	
22nd	Field Ambulance left WINNEZEELE and returned to Farm at WIPPENHOEK. "C" Section proceeded to by bus YPRES, for duty reporting there at 8.30 p.m. "Boy Scout" Motor Ambulance Car with personnel – 1 N.C.O. & men RAMC and two others – attached Lieut CRONIN returned.	
24th	Further 25% of blankets overhauled. Casualties dealt with at YPRES and handed to 85th Field Ambulance, therefore not put through admission and discharge Book of this Field Ambulance. Wounded 150. Total 214.	
	Sick 24. + 40. Wounded.	

Army Form C. 2118.

WAR DIARY
INTELLIGENCE SUMMARY.
(Erase heading not required.)

8th (2nd London) Field Ambulance
28th Division.

Hour, Date, Place	Summary of Events and Information	Remarks and references to Appendices
MAY 1915		
25th	At midday received orders to leave WIPPENHOEK Farm, and proceed to LYSSENHOEK Farm Rly cg map 27 Belgium L.2.9.C, and be clear by 3 pm as Headquarters Northumbrian Division required WIPPENHOEK Farm. Casualties: Sick 50, Gun 157 Wounded 429 Total 636.	
26th	"B" section proceeded to Asylum YPRES to relieve "C" section	
26th	Capt RAWES sent to Hospital. Casualties: Sick 19, GasI35 Wounded 145 Total 199.	
27th	Undergoing determination of Officers, no/Operations received Casualties: Sick 21. Gas 4. Wounded 69 Total 94	
28th	Casualties - Sick 28, Gas I. Wounded 85. Total 114.	
29th	Handed over Asylum to 9th Field Ambulance, "C" section proceeded to detached WINNEZEELE to take over from Northumbrian Field Ambulance, and camp on Brigade Hospital. Lieut GRIFFITH E.W arrived	
30th	Unit less above proceeded to LE TEMPLE near WINNEZEELE	

Wm Salisbury Sharpe
Lt Col

12/5193

28th Division

84th Field Ambulance

Vol VI

Auto

12/5193

June 1915.

3 sheets

Army Form C. 2118.

5th (2 London) Field Ambulance
28th Division

WAR DIARY
or
INTELLIGENCE SUMMARY.
(Erase heading not required.)

Instructions regarding War Diaries and Intelligence Summaries are contained in F.S. Regs., Part II. and the Staff Manual respectively. Title pages will be prepared in manuscript.

Hour, Date, Place		Summary of Events and Information	Remarks and references to Appendices
WINNEZEELE	1	Casualties :- Sick 1	
June 1915	2	Lieut McLAGGAN detailed for duty with 3rd Royal Fusiliers vice Lieut STEELE to this Unit. Casualties - Sick 1.	
		Tent Hospital opened at LE CROOG Farm.	
	3	Casualties :- Sick 12.	
	4	Do. Sick 13	
	5	Do. Sick 13 — Inspection by A.D.M.S. 28th Divn	
	6	Do. Sick 7 Inspection by G.O.C 28th Divn	
	7	Do. Sick 13	
	8	Do. Sick 15. Special Sanitary machines received and issued.	
		Draft 3 men received	
	9	Casualties :- Sick 19	
	10	Do. Sick 14, Wounded 17 (Hand grenades)	
	11	Do. Sick 9.	
	12	Do. Sick 10. Wounded 2.	
	13	Received order to move to LA CLYTTE.	

3 Sheets

Army Form C. 2118.

84th (2/London) Field Ambulance
28th Division

WAR DIARY
or
INTELLIGENCE SUMMARY.
(Erase heading not required.)

Instructions regarding War Diaries and Intelligence Summaries are contained in F.S. Regs., Part II. and the Staff Manual respectively. Title pages will be prepared in manuscript.

Hour, Date, Place	Summary of Events and Information	Remarks and references to Appendices
June 14 1915	Unit moved to LA CLYTTE. Took over School buildings and huts as Hospital from 43rd Field Ambulance. Casualties :- Wounded 9, Sick 5.	
15	Lieut GRIFFITH sent to 31st Brigade R.F.A. vice Lieut MACCONACHY - to this Unit for duty. Casualties - Sick 29, Wounded 7.	
16	do .. Sick 33, Wounded 6. Lieut CRONIN sent to 1st Suffolks for temporary duty as M/O.	
17	Lieut BAXTER to 2nd Northumberland Fusiliers vice Lieut COWAN - wounded. Casualties :- Sick 33, Wounded 16.	
18	Casualties :- Sick 21, Wounded 13.	
19	do - Sick 37, Wounded 6.	
20	Lieut BAXTER rejoined. Casualties - Sick 14 Wounded 17.	
21	Additional Motor Transport driver joined. Advanced Dressing Station established at Mt MIKERIS at DICKEBUSCH. Casualties :- Sick 30, Wounded 9.	

(73989) W4141—463. 400,000. 9/14. H.&J.Ltd. Forms/C. 2118/10.

3 Sheets

Army Form C. 2118.

WAR DIARY
or
INTELLIGENCE SUMMARY.
(Erase heading not required.)

8th (2 London) Field Ambulance,
28th Division

Instructions regarding War Diaries and Intelligence Summaries are contained in F.S. Regs., Part II and the Staff Manual respectively. Title pages will be prepared in manuscript.

Hour, Date, Place 1915.	Summary of Events and Information	Remarks and references to Appendices
June 22	20 men sent to BASSAYE as working party, to assist in building dug-out dressing station.	
23	Casualties - Sick 25. Wounded 15.	
	Do :- Sick 37. Wounded 14. Lieut. CRONIN rejoined.	
	Lieut. DOBBIE joined. Hospital taken over entirely by "B" section.	
24	Casualties - Sick 32. Wounded 7.	
25	Do - Sick 43. Wounded 10	
26	Do - Sick 44. Wounded 16	
27	Lieut DOBBIE detailed to 3rd Brigade R.F.A.	
	D.D.M.S. II Corps inspected Field Ambulance.	
	Casualties - Sick 63. Wounded 20.	
28	Lieut MACCONACHY transferred to 1st Division.	
	Casualties - Sick 37. Wounded 9.	
29	Do - Sick 52. Wounded 25.	
30	Do - Sick 32. Wounded 7. Army 1st met on parade.	

Wm Malcolm Shanks
Col

121/6443

28th Division

84th Field Ambulance

Part VII

From 1st to 31st July 1915

12/6443

July /15

Army Form C. 2118.

WAR DIARY
or
INTELLIGENCE SUMMARY.   84th (2nd London T) Field Ambulance
(Erase heading not required.)

Instructions regarding War Diaries and Intelligence Summaries are contained in F.S. Regs., Part II. and the Staff Manual respectively. Title pages will be prepared in manuscript.

Hour, Date, Place		Summary of Events and Information	Remarks and references to Appendices
LA CLYTTE July 1915	1.	Lieut FORREST found doctors nearest enemy rifles. Casualties :- Sick 30. Wounded 21.	
	2.	ADMS 28th Division inspected the Transport of this Unit. Inspection on the whole satisfactory, but to dislodge several points rather further knowledge of gun and cart and required, particularly on the part of Wagon Orderlies. Casualties - Sick 40. Wounded 14.	
	3.	Lieut LAWSON to 31st Bde R.F.A. vice Lieut GRIFFITH sick. Casualties: Sick 54. Wounded 19.	
	4.	"Bay Scout" Motor Ambulance Car with personnel attached to this unit sent to DICKEBUSH to Advance Dressing Station to relieve party there. Casualties - Sick 35. Wounded 15.	
	5.	List of men sent to DDMS II Corps stating their qualifications as dental mechanics, laboratory attendants, chemical or bacteriological, men with knowledge of biography and electrotherapy. Casualties :- Sick 53. Wounded 10.	

Army Form C. 2118.

WAR DIARY
or
INTELLIGENCE SUMMARY.   84th (2nd London T) Field Ambulance
(Erase heading not required.)

Instructions regarding War Diaries and Intelligence Summaries are contained in F. S. Regs., Part II and the Staff Manual respectively. Title pages will be prepared in manuscript.

Hour, Date, Place	Summary of Events and Information	Remarks and references to Appendices
1915 July 6.	Casualties - Sick 33. Wounded 15.	
7.	Lieut HAIG joined. Lieut STEELE sent to 2 KOR Lanc. Lieut FORREST to Monmouth Regt. Casualties - Sick 36, Wounded 23.	
8.	do - Sick 26, Wounded 21.	
9.	do - Sick 36, Wounded 28.	
10.	Orders received concerning self-inflicted wounds. Casualties - Sick 25. Wounded 27. 2/C.S. SHARPE to Mont Noir sick.	
11.	Lieut. HARWOOD to Mont Noir sick. Lieut LAWSON rejoined. Casualties - Sick 18. Wounded 17.	
12.	C section moved to ST HUBERTUSHOEK from area DICKEBUSH. Casualties - Sick 24. Wounded 20.	
13.	E section shelled at ST HUBERTUSHOEK, two tents damaged but no men injured. Casualties - Sick 39. Wounded 9.	

WAR DIARY or INTELLIGENCE SUMMARY.

Army Form C. 2118.

84 H(2 London T.) Field Ambulance

Hour, Date, Place	Summary of Events and Information	Remarks and references to Appendices
July 14.	Lieut. STEELE rejoined. Casualties:- Sick 412, Wounded 29.	
15.	Lt.Col. SHARPE rejoined. "C" section returned. Orders received to move tomorrow. Casualties:- Sick 28 Wounded 14.	
BOESCHEPE 16.	Field Amb^{ce} moved to a farm between BOESCHEPE and BERTHEN, taking over personal Post Motor thre from 86th Field Amb^{ce}. 193 patients taken over. ADMS visited the D.R.S. immediately on our arrival. "B" section at LA CLYTTE handed over to 86th Field Amb^{ce}. Admissions at D.R.S. Sick 4.	
17	"B" section moved to DRANOUTRE to establish an Advanced Station, taking over from 3rd Northumbrian Field Amb^{ce}. Casualties:- Evacuy Stn:- Sick 2 Wounded 4. D.R.S. Sick 24. Wounded 2.	
18	Casualties:- Evacuy Stn. Sick 25 Wounded 22. D.R.S. " 14 " 2. PTE SELL relieve Sick.	
19.	Casualties. Evacuy Stn. Sick 42 Wounded 9. D.R.S. " " 15 " 14	

Army Form C. 2118.

WAR DIARY
or
INTELLIGENCE SUMMARY.
(Erase heading not required.)

4th (2nd London T) Field Ambulance

Hour, Date, Place	Summary of Events and Information	Remarks and references to Appendices
July 20. 1915	Motor-bus Kay wounded. Inspection and classification by Veterinary Officer. Dressing Stn. Sick 16. Wounded 6. Casualties D.R.S. Sick 47.	
21	Casualties - Dressing Stn. Sick 11. Wounded 7 to - D.R.S. " 25.	
22	Genl HAIG inspected Local Cars with horses L.A.M.B. and DENAGY joined. Casualties - Dressing Stn. Sick 16. Wounded 1. D.R.S. Sick 39. Wounded 1.	
23	Casualties - Dressing Stn. Sick 22. Wounded 9. D.R.S. " 15.	
24	Rev W.B HOGG Church of England Chaplain attached to Unit at DRANOUTRE. Casualties - Dressing Stn. Sick 14. Wounded 13. D.R.S. " 16. " 2.	

Army Form C. 2118.

WAR DIARY
or
INTELLIGENCE SUMMARY.
(Erase heading not required.)

Instructions regarding War Diaries and Intelligence Summaries are contained in F. S. Regs., Part II. and the Staff Manual respectively. Title pages will be prepared in manuscript.

6th M (2 nd London T) Field Ambulance

Hour, Date, Place	Summary of Events and Information	Remarks and references to Appendices
July 25 1915	Pte P.G. MITCHELL sent to A.D.M.S. Office. Casualties :— Evacuation Station Sick 16 Wounded 8 A.R.S. 22	
26	Lieut HARWOOD rejoined. O.R.S. inspected by D.D.M.S. 2 Corps. Casualties :— Evacuation Station Sick 14 Wounded 13 A.R.S. 42	
27	Lieut CRONIN sent to C.C.S. with injured arm. Casualties :— Evacuation Station Sick 13 Wounded 19 A.R.S. 45 " 2	
28	Casualties :— Evacuation Station Sick 18 Wounded 17 A.R.S. 31 " 3	
29	Casualties :— Evacuation Stn Sick 14 Wounded 3 A.R.S. 24 " 3	
30	Lieut ELKINGTON rejoined. Casualties :— Evacuation Stn Sick 25 Wounded 17 A.R.S. 19 " 1	
31	Casualties :— Evacuation Stn. Sick 18 Wounded 8 A.R.S. 12	

W. L. Salusbury Hughes
Lt. Col.

12/6857

28th Division

8th Field Ambulance

Polsent

August 15

August 1915

Army Form C. 2118.

WAR DIARY
or
INTELLIGENCE SUMMARY.
(Erase heading not required.)

3/10 (2nd London T) Field Ambulance
R.A.M.C.

Instructions regarding War Diaries and Intelligence Summaries are contained in F.S. Regs., Part II. and the Staff Manual respectively. Title pages will be prepared in manuscript.

Hour, Date, Place	Summary of Events and Information	Remarks and references to Appendices
1st August 1915.	Lieut ENINSON, R.F. joined.	
	CASUALTIES Admissions to Field Ambce. O.R. Sick 11 Wounded 2, D.R.S. O.R. Sick 13.	
2nd August 1915.	CASUALTIES Admissions to Field Ambce. O. Sick 1 O.R. Sick 13 Wounded 6. D.R.S. O.R. S.20 W.1.	
3rd August 1915.	CASUALTIES Admissions to Field Ambce. O. W.1 O.R. S.11 W.3. D.R.S. O.R. S.21	
4th August 1915.	"A" Section Bearers and Sergeant Major under Lieut LAWSON proceeded to DRANOUTRE.	
5th August 1915.	CASUALTIES Admns. to Fd Amb. O. Sick 1. O.R. Sick 12. D.R.S. O.R. S.30 W.1	
	CASUALTIES " " " O.R. S.13. W.8. D.R.S. O.R. S.31 W.2.	
6th August 1915.	Capt McQUEEN joined.	
	CASUALTIES Admns to Fd Amb. O. S.1. O.R. S.19. D.R.S. O.R. S.22 W.2.	
7th August 1915.	CASUALTIES " " " O.R. S.13. W.4. D.R.S. O.R. S.22 W.1	
8th August 1915.	CASUALTIES " " " O. S.1. W.1. O.R. S.9. W.9. D.R.S. O.R. S.26.	
9th August 1915.	Lieut ENINSON to 28th D.A.C. for temp. duty.	
	CASUALTIES Admns to Fd Amb. O.R. S.13. W.21. D.R.S. O.R. S.21 W.1.	

Army Form C. 2118.

WAR DIARY
or
INTELLIGENCE SUMMARY.
(Erase heading not required.)

8ᵗʰ (2ⁿᵈ London T.) Field Ambulance RAMC.

Instructions regarding War Diaries and Intelligence Summaries are contained in F.S. Regs., Part II. and the Staff Manual respectively. Title pages will be prepared in manuscript.

Hour, Date, Place	Summary of Events and Information	Remarks and references to Appendices
10ᵗʰ August 1915	Lieut HAIG to 140ᵗʰ Division. Two Officers two N.C.Os and ten men of the 108ᵗʰ F. Amb. reported for instruction at D.R.S. and a similar number to B Section. (168 hours instruction at each place). CASUALTIES Admns to Totnl. O. S1. OR. S19. w.5 DRS OR S 34 w 2	
11ᵗʰ August 1915.	Lieut ELKINGTON to 2ⁿᵈ Cheshire Regt. for temp. duty. Surgeon Gen. PORTER inspected DRS. CASUALTIES admns to Totnl OR. S16 w 8. DRS OR S28 w.2	
12ᵗʰ August 1915.	G.O.C. 2ⁿᵈ ARMY inspected DRS. CASUALTIES admns to Totnl O. S1. OR. S16. w.9. DRS OR S24 w.2	
13ᵗʰ August 1915	" " " O w.2. OR S11. w.5. DRS OR S.35	
14ᵗʰ August 1915	cl Justin two officers two N.C.Os and ten men of 8ᵗʰ Field amb. at D.R.S. and B Section for instruction CASUALTIES admns to Totnl OR S.21 w 6. DRS OR S31 w.2	

Army Form C. 2118.

WAR DIARY
or
INTELLIGENCE SUMMARY.
(Erase heading not required.)

8th (2nd London T.) Field Ambulance
R.A.M.C.

Instructions regarding War Diaries and Intelligence Summaries are contained in F.S. Regs., Part II. and the Staff Manual respectively. Title pages will be prepared in manuscript.

Hour, Date, Place	Summary of Events and Information	Remarks and references to Appendices
15th August 1915.	CASUALTIES admn. to Hosptl. O. S1 W1. OR. S 13 W 5. DRS. OR. S21 W1.	
16th August 1915	CASUALTIES " " OR. S 16 W.25 DRS. OR. S 34 W 3.	
17th August 1915.	CASUALTIES " " OR. S. 35 W 19. DRS OR. S.35 W 3.	
18th August 1915	Draft of two men received from BASE. A further party of 108 " L.dnl. for instruction at DRS. and B Section	
	CASUALTIES admn. to Hosptl. O. W 1. OR. S.20 W 2. DRS. OR. S. 27 W 5.	
19th August 1915.	Capt HAYNES. returned to Unit from England OR. S 15 W 7. DRS. OR.S. 22.	
20th August 1915	CASUALTIES admn. to Hosptl. " " O. S. 1. OR. S 14 W 3. DRS OR. S. 30. W 1	
21st August 1915	CASUALTIES " " OR. S.4. W 10. DRS. OR. S. 34 W 3.	
22nd August 1915.	CASUALTIES " " O. W 1. OR. S. 10. W 8. DRS. OR. S. 30. W 5	

Army Form C. 2118.

WAR DIARY
or
INTELLIGENCE SUMMARY.
(Erase heading not required.)

8th (2nd London) Field Ambulance. R.A.M.C.

Hour, Date, Place	Summary of Events and Information	Remarks and references to Appendices
23rd August 1915	Capt McQUEEN to 3rd Monmouth Regt. for temp. duty. Important orders and instructions received from 2nd Corps, for evacuating patients and care of and storing equipment, in case Field Amb. goes into action. CASUALTIES. Column & Tetnl. O.R. S. 21. W.6. DRS. O.R. S. 19 W.1	
24th August 1915	CASUALTIES " " O. S.1. O.R. S.14. W.6. DRS. O.R. S. 29 W.3	
25th August 1915	Lieut R.V. STEELE to 3rd Monmouth Regt. vice Capt. McQUEEN. CASUALTIES Column & Tetnl. O.R. S. 13. W.1. DRS.O.R.S. 36 W.2.	
26th August 1915	CASUALTIES " " O. S.3. O.R. S. 10. W.4. O.R. DRS. S. 24. W.5.	
27th August 1915	Pte MITCHELL returned to Unit from temp. work at ADMS Office. Lieut STEELE returned from 3rd Monmouth Regt. CASUALTIES Column & Tetnl. O. S.1. W.1. O.R. S.9. W.3. DRS. O.R. S. 20.	

Army Form C. 2118.

WAR DIARY
or
INTELLIGENCE SUMMARY.

3rd (2 London. T) Field amb.
R.A.M.C.

(Erase heading not required.)

Instructions regarding War Diaries and Intelligence Summaries are contained in F.S. Regs., Part II. and the Staff Manual respectively. Title pages will be prepared in manuscript.

Hour, Date, Place	Summary of Events and Information	Remarks and references to Appendices
28th August 1915	CASUALTIES Admno to hospl O.R. S.9 W.6 DRS. OR S.19.	
29th August 1915	CASUALTIES " " O S.I. OR. S. 12. W.5. DRS OR S.27. Lieut BAXTER to hos- Held for temp duty.	
30th August 1915	CASUALTIES admno to hospl O.S.I. OR S12 W.3. DRS. OR S. 29 W.1.	
31st August 1915	Enquiry received asking of any men proved any thoring in Engineering qualification CASUALTIES admno to hospl. O.W.1. OR.S.9. W 10. DRS,O.R. S. 27.	WmWalsburyShaye L.Col

(73989) W4141—463. 400,000. 9/14. H.&J.Ltd. Forms/C. 2118/10.

121/7183

38th Koroop....

84th Field Ambulance

Vol ix.

Sep 1/15

Army Form C. 2118.

84th (2nd London T) Field Ambulance Return
in the Field

WAR DIARY
or
INTELLIGENCE SUMMARY.
(Erase heading not required.)

Instructions regarding War Diaries and Intelligence Summaries are contained in F.S. Regs., Part II. and the Staff Manual respectively. Title pages will be prepared in manuscript.

Hour, Date, Place	Summary of Events and Information	Remarks and references to Appendices
1st September 1915.	C/o 39. Pte BRISCOE G.G. proceeded to CADET SCHOOL, BLENDECQUES for training for T. Commission. Admissions to Field amb. Officers Nil. O'Rank. 8 sick. 8 wounded " " Divisional Rest Station O'Ranks 22 do 1 do	
2nd September 1915.	Admissions to Field amb. Officer Nil. O'Ranks 8 sick 1 wounded " " D.R.S. O'Ranks 23 do 3 do	
3rd September 1915.	Army Order XIV August 1915. received. "National Health Insurance Contributions". Admissions to Field amb. Officers Nil. O'Rank 140 sick 2 wounded " " D.R.S. do 38 do do do	
4th September 1915.	Admissions to Field amb. Officers 1 sick. O'Rank. 17 sick 1 wounded " " D.R.S. do 20 do 1 do	
5th September 1915.	Admissions to Field amb. Officers 1 sick. O'Rank 16 sick 6 wounded " " D.R.S. O'Rank. 52 do 1 do	
6th September 1915.	C/o 83 Sgt PUTLAND E. to Hospital BASE for treatment. Admissions to Field amb. Officers Nil. O'Ranks. 13 sick 5 wounded " " D.R.S. O'Ranks 140 do Nil do	

(73989) W4141—463. 400,000. 9/14. H.&J.Ltd. Forms/C. 2118/10.

Army Form C. 2118.

No "(2nd London T) Field Ambulance RAMC
& the Field

WAR DIARY
or
INTELLIGENCE SUMMARY.
(Erase heading not required.)

Instructions regarding War Diaries and Intelligence Summaries are contained in F. S. Regs., Part II. and the Staff Manual respectively. Title pages will be prepared in manuscript.

Hour, Date, Place	Summary of Events and Information	Remarks and references to Appendices
7th September 1915	Rev H.V. FARNFIELD, Rev J. FIRTH and Partner proceeded to 53rd Brigade. C/O 366 Pte BURRELL F.G. to C/o 4 Stationary Hospital, ARQUES, for duty as Dental attendant. Admissions to Total Officers Nil. Other Ranks 16 each 5 wounded & D.R.S. do 18 do 2 do	
8th September 1915	Admissions to H.Hosp Officers Nil. Other Ranks 11 each 5 wounded & D.R.S. do 21 do Nil do	
9th September 1915	Special R.O. 192 "Tube Helmets" received. C/o 242 Cpl WHITE F.R. to 28 London Regt for training in view of T. Com. other Ranks 13 each 1 wounded Admissions to Total Officers Nil do 20 do 2 do & D.R.S.	
10th September 1915	Admissions to Total Officers Nil Other Ranks 13 each 16 wounded & D.R.S. do 29 do Nil do	
11th September 1915	Admissions to Total Officers Nil Other Ranks 15 each 2 wounded & D.R.S. do 21 do Nil do	
12th September 1915	Admissions to Total Officers Nil Other Ranks 16 each 4 wounded & D.R.S. do 26 do 2 do	

Army Form C. 2118.

WAR DIARY
or
INTELLIGENCE SUMMARY.
(Erase heading not required.)

3/10 (2nd London T.) Field Ambulance R.A.M.C.
In the Field

Hour, Date, Place	Summary of Events and Information	Remarks and references to Appendices
13th September 1915	C/o 109 Pte LAWE A.G proceeded to England to take up Commission in 3rd Dorset Regt. No. 1034 A/Cpl COLEMAN M C/o 1035 A/Cpl HINCE E and No. 1036 Dvr MANDY E. proceeded to BASE preparatory to discharge to Field and. Officers 1 sick 1 Wounded O.Ranks 17 sick 10 wounded Admission to D.R.S. 20 do Nil do	
16th September 1915.	6 Field Amb. Officers Nil Other Ranks 18 sick 3 wounded Admissions to D.R.S. do 23 do 3 do	
15th September 1915	Admissions to Total Officers 1 wounded. Other Ranks 110 sick 9 wounded to D.R.S. do 17 do 2 do	
16th September 1915	Lieut WEBB, H. joined Admissions to Total Officers 2 wounded Other Ranks 14 sick 8 wounded to D.R.S. do 20 do 1 do	
17th September 1915	Admissions to Total Officers Nil Other Ranks 14 sick 3 wounded to D.R.S. do 20 do 1 do	
18th September 1915	Admissions to Total Officers 1 sick Other Ranks 4 sick 12 wounded to D.R.S. do 4/10 do 4 do do	

Army Form C. 2118.

WAR DIARY
or
INTELLIGENCE SUMMARY.
(Erase heading not required.)

 $3/b^{th}$ (2/1 London T.) Field Ambulance
TRAMS
In the Field

Instructions regarding War Diaries and Intelligence Summaries are contained in F.S. Regs., Part II. and the Staff Manual respectively. Title pages will be prepared in manuscript.

Hour, Date, Place	Summary of Events and Information	Remarks and references to Appendices
19th September 1915	Report asked for of mechanics suitable for transfer to R. Flying Corps. CAPT. HOGG W.B. (CF Chaplain) to Hospital (sick). Admissions to total, Officers Nil. Other Ranks 10 sick, 5 wounded. do do do 7 do Nil do 6 D.R.S.	
20th September 1915	Canadians arrived to take over D.R.S. Admissions to total Officers Nil. Other Ranks 12 sick, 1 wounded to 19 do. Y. d. 6 D.R.S.	
21st September 1915	A Section bearers under CAPT. LAWSON returned to Roesinghe. 1 Ambulance from ZWYNE BAK. Four men remained at ZWYNECOCK and two at the Advanced Dressing Station, until Canadian arrived when they returned to B Section under the orders of Major MONTGOMERY SMITH. LIEUT BAXTER W returned from Temp. duty with 1st WELSH REG. LIEUT WEBB H. to 1st SUFFOLK REGT as M.O. t/c Admission to Total Officers 2 sick. Other Ranks 12 sick, 6 wounded do 20 do. 3 do 6 D.R.S.	

Army Form C. 2118.

WAR DIARY
or
INTELLIGENCE SUMMARY.

(Erase heading not required.)

3rd (2nd London T.) Field Ambulance
Little Hied   FRANCE

Instructions regarding War Diaries and Intelligence Summaries are contained in F.S. Regs., Part II and the Staff Manual respectively. Title pages will be prepared in manuscript.

Hour, Date, Place	Summary of Events and Information	Remarks and references to Appendices
22nd September 1915	Canadians took over from B Section at DRANOUTRE. Admissions } Total NIL } 6 DRS. NIL.	
23rd September 1915	Canadians took over DRS. The Unit, complete, moved to new Brigade area. Headquarters at LA BELLE CROIX, B Section at FERME LA SAGE, C Section at Hospital party at VANDEVELDE farm & the Brigade ad hospital of injured. (B Section marched from DRANOUTRE under Major MONTGOMERY SMITH, and the other ambulance bow marched separately with M.A.W. Unit under Lieut HEWITT.) Orders given for readiness for move at 10.0 a.m. 24.9.15. No 127 Pte JONES E reported to 28 Division train vice No 238 Pte JELLY H. returned to duty with that on other Golic CAPT FARNFIELD and CAPT FIRTH (Riflemen) and Relvers returned from 13th Brigade Admissions to Total. Other Ranks 2 sick	

(73989) W 4141-463. 400,000. 9/14. H.&J.Ltd. Forms/C. 2118/10.

Army Form C. 2118.

WAR DIARY
or
INTELLIGENCE SUMMARY.
(Erase heading not required.)

86th (2nd London T) Field Ambulance RAMC
In the Field.

Instructions regarding War Diaries and Intelligence Summaries are contained in F.S. Regs., Part II. and the Staff Manual respectively. Title pages will be prepared in manuscript.

Hour, Date, Place	Summary of Events and Information	Remarks and references to Appendices
24th September 1915.	The remainder of Ambulance moved to VANDEVELDE Farm. Special Orders given for readiness for move. C/o 184 Pte PEEK H.S. } to 2/8 London Regt, for training for T. Comm. " 204 " BREESE M.C. } " 936 Cpl FOLEATE .P. } returned to Divisional Train. T1/036601 Dvr. GREEN A.G. } Admissions to L.of.C. 12. each Other Ranks.	
25th September 1915.	Special orders received, to be ready for move if ordered. Admissions to Total Other Ranks 9 sick.	
26th September 1915.	The Unit complete marched with 83rd Brigade to ROBECQ. A Section Tent party opened Hospital for Brigade sick. Admissions to L.of.C. Other Ranks 24 each.	
27th September 1915.	Unit moved to VERQUIGNEUL. C Section proceeded by lorries. Every m.td. Brigade to open Dressing Station if necessary. Admissions to Field Amb. NIL	

Army Form C. 2118.

WAR DIARY
or
INTELLIGENCE SUMMARY.
(Erase heading not required.)

St H- (2nd London T) Field Amb. RAMC
In the Field.

Hour, Date, Place	Summary of Events and Information	Remarks and references to Appendices
28" September 1915	Admission to Hotoul Nil.	
29" September 1915	A Section Left Sub Division and C Section complete moved to COLLEGE de JEUNES FILLES, BETHUNE. B Section complete and A Section bearers proceeded to VERMELLES and opened Dressing Station. Admission to Hotoul. Nil.	
30" September 1915	The Hospital at COLLEGE de JEUNES FILLES taken over from C/O 26. Field Ambulance. No 296. Pte RUSSELL A.L. Wounded to BASE. CAPT. H.M. STRATFORD joined from England. Admission to Hotoul- Officers 2 wounded Other Ranks 4/ sick and 16/ wounded	

W. Salusbury Trevor
Lt Col

St (2nd lieut) J. Auld
———————
See
Vol XI

Army Form C. 2118.

4/1 (2nd London T.) Field Ambulance
B.E.F.

WAR DIARY
or
INTELLIGENCE SUMMARY.
(Erase heading not required.)

Instructions regarding War Diaries and Intelligence Summaries are contained in F.S. Regs., Part II. and the Staff Manual respectively. Title pages will be prepared in manuscript.

Hour, Date, Place	Summary of Events and Information	Remarks and references to Appendices
1st Oct. 1915.	Reinforcement of other rank from BASE. No 53094 Pte PEAK W.H. proceeded to England to take up Temp. Commission. CASUALTIES. Admissions to Hospl. Other Ranks 4 sick 110 wounded.	
2 Oct 1915.	B Section complete and A Section bearers joined Headquarters at CALAESE de JENNES FALLES BETHUNE. Capt Haynes returned to England. No 4016 Pte GOLDSMITH C. killed in action. No 316 and 307 Pte GURNEY G.F. and MILLER.T. departed in action. No 68 Sergt. A/Cpl. HENDERSON.R. promoted to Sergt A/Cpl. CASUALTIES. Admissions O.R. 3 sick 29 wounded.	
3rd Oct 1915.	Lieut. Lenert with 26 Bearers and 3 Other ORs Cars proceed to Queens, CAMBRIN to escort 86 Field Amb. in clearing wounded. Admissions O.R. 19 sick 11 wounded.	

(73989) W.4141-463. 400,000. 9/14. H.&J.Ltd. Forms/C. 2118/10.

Army Form C. 2118.

WAR DIARY
or
INTELLIGENCE SUMMARY.
(Erase heading not required.)

Co. = (2nd London T.) Field Ambulance
R.A.M.C.

Instructions regarding War Diaries and Intelligence Summaries are contained in F. S. Regs., Part II. and the Staff Manual respectively. Title pages will be prepared in manuscript.

Hour, Date, Place	Summary of Events and Information	Remarks and references to Appendices
4th Oct 1915	Admissions Officer 1 wounded. O.R. 9 sick 16 wounded	
5th Oct 1915	Admissions O.R. 6 sick.	
6th Oct 1915	The Unit complete proceeded GONNEHEM (Resting area)	
	Capt. (Rev) F. H DRINKWATER to N.1. HOSPITAL wounded	
	Admissions O.R. 6 sick.	
7th Oct 1915		
8th Oct 1915	Draft of 1 man (saddler) received from BASE	
	Admissions O.R. 12 sick. 1 wounded	
9th Oct 1915	Admissions Officer 1 wounded. O.R. 16 sick	
10th Oct 1915	Admissions O.R. 7 sick 1 wounded	
	Lieut BAXTER.W promoted to T. CAPT.	
11th Oct 1915	Capt. R. McQUEEN attached for duty.	
	Draft of three men received from BASE	
	Admissions OFFICERS 2. SICK. O.R. 9 SICK	

Army Form C. 2118.

WAR DIARY
or
INTELLIGENCE SUMMARY.
(Erase heading not required.)

Instructions regarding War Diaries and Intelligence Summaries are contained in F. S. Regs., Part II. and the Staff Manual respectively. Title pages will be prepared in manuscript.

Hour, Date, Place	Summary of Events and Information	Remarks and references to Appendices
12th Oct. 1915	Admissions O.R. 10. Sick.	
13th Oct. 1915	Capt. R. McQueen L. 28th Div. Amm. Column as M.O. 4c. Sgt. James and 12 bearers proceeded to VERMELLES to await 16th Division Advanced Dressing Station. Admissions Officer 1 Sick O.R. 1 Sick & Wounded.	
14th Oct. 1915	Stretcher party at VERMELLES relieved by party under Sgt. Baker. Admissions O.R. 9 Sick 2 Wounded.	
15th Oct. 1915	Sgt. Baker and party returned from VERMELLES. Admissions Officer 1 Sick 1 Wounded O.R. 15. Sick	
16th Oct. 1915	Unit moved to BETHUNE and took over Civil and Military Hospital from 21st Field Ambulance, also stretcher bearers under Sgt. Wheeler proceeded to Dressing Station. Lieut. W.B. Graham joined. Capt. J.I. Lawson L. 2 K.O.R. Lancs as M.O. 4c. Admissions O.R. 1. Sick.	

(73989) W4141—463. 400,000. 9/14. H.&J.Ltd. Forms/C. 2118/10.

Army Form C. 2118.

WAR DIARY
or
INTELLIGENCE SUMMARY.
(Erase heading not required.)

Instructions regarding War Diaries and Intelligence Summaries are contained in F.S. Regs., Part II. and the Staff Manual respectively. Title pages will be prepared in manuscript.

Hour, Date, Place	Summary of Events and Information	Remarks and references to Appendices
17th October 1915	A Section less Headquarters duties proceeded to Advanced Dressing at BUSBURE near GIVENCHY-LEZ-LA-BASSEE.	
	Admissions :- O.R. 8 SICK.	
18th October 1915	Admissions :- O.R. 19 SICK 18 WOUNDED	
19th October 1915	Admissions :- O.R. 11 SICK 4 WOUNDED	
20th October 1915	21 Heavy Draught Horses handed over to R.F.A. and 62 light Draught received in place. 10 R.F.A. men sent to Unit as drivers until A.S.C. men arrived. Blanket limbers complete with horses and personnel returned to Divisional Train. Motor Ambulance bars and drivers exchanged for SUNBEAM withdrawn. Cars with Nos 5 and 6. Field Ambulances.	
	Admissions :- O.R. 36 SICK. 12 WOUNDED.	
21st October 1915.	Unit moved to FORNEHEM. Draft of 13 A.S.C. men received in relief of R.F.A. drivers.	
	Admissions :- O.R. 6 SICK 4 WOUNDED.	

Army Form C. 2118.

WAR DIARY
or
INTELLIGENCE SUMMARY.
(Erase heading not required.)

Instructions regarding War Diaries and Intelligence Summaries are contained in F. S. Regs., Part II. and the Staff Manual respectively. Title pages will be prepared in manuscript.

Hour, Date, Place	Summary of Events and Information	Remarks and references to Appendices
22nd October 1915	Admissions. OR. 26. SICK. 1. WOUNDED.	
23rd October 1915	Unit marched to KILLERS. for entrainment to MARSEILLES. Entrained at 10.51 p.m. Admissions: NIL	
24th October 1915	Unit in train. Admissions: NIL	
25th October 1915	ditto	
26th October 1915	Unit arrived at MARSEILLES at 3.30 a.m. and marched to PARC BORELLY Camp. Capt BICKERTON and 100 men embarked on "SS HALDA" Admissions :- NIL	
27th October 1915	Admissions: NIL	
28th October 1915	Admissions: NIL	
29th October 1915	O.C. and CAPT FIRTH and 66 men embarked on S.S. "KAROA" Admissions:- NIL	
30th October 1915		
31st October 1915	S.S. "KAROA" sailed at 6.30 a.m. Admissions: OR 2 SICK.	

(73989) W.4141—463. 400,000. 9/14. H.&J.Ltd. Forms/C. 2118/10.

www.ingramcontent.com/pod-product-compliance
Lightning Source LLC
Chambersburg PA
CBHW081245170426
43191CB00034B/2046